The Copts
In
Twenty Centuries

A short History

Elham Khalil

Based on the Audio history-exhibition production
"Kemet"
Written and produced by Elham Khalil
For The Coptic Museum
Ruinerworld
Netherlands
1999-2006

Egypt during the Greek, Roman, Byzantine and Arab-Islamic rulers

To the enduring spirit
of
The Copts
Throughout History

"Who shall separate us
from the love of Christ?
shall tribulation, or distress,
or persecution, or famine,
or nakedness, or peril, or sword?
As it is written,
For thy sake we are killed all the day long;
we are accounted as sheep for the slaughter.
Nay, in all these things we are more than
conquerors through him that loved us.
For I am persuaded, that neither death,
nor life, nor angels,
nor principalities, nor powers,
nor things present, nor things to come,
Nor height, nor depth,
nor any other creature,
shall be able to separate us
from the love of God,
which is in Christ Jesus our Lord."

Romans 1 35-39

Elham Khalil was born in 1947, Asyut, Egypt, and lives since 1970 in the Netherlands. She studied English language and literature at Cairo University and got her Dorctoral degree in Anglo-Irish Drama from Amsterdam University in 1976. Obtained her PhD Social Sciences and International Communication from Amsterdam University in 1983.

Worked for years as senior broadcaster, producer, newsreader and reporter for the Dutch Foreign Broadcasting in Hilversum. Lived on and managed the family farm in the Dutch Veluwe countryside between 1978 and 2010.

Established and managed the Coptic Museum in Ruinerwold, between 2000 and 2006.

Attended drama courses at Exeter College, Oxford University between 2004 and 2006.

Her love for stage started in her teens and she never stopped writing plays since then. Only at the end of 2009 it was possible to start publishing her plays, short stories and her writings on the Coptic history, church and culture.

Elham Khalil has two daughters.

Welcome in Kemet
The Egyptians called their country "Kemet"
"the Black Soil"

The word Copt means Egyptian (Egyptos).

The Egyptians were the first people on earth to create a nation-state.

State, religion and culture formed an indisputable unity. Herodotus, the Greek Historian who travelled some 500 years before Christ described the Egyptians as the most religious people on earth. Their religious background helped them to accept Christianity with eagerness and to enjoy its depth through their ascetic life, meditation and studying of the Holy Scripture.

For nearly one thousand years of Greek and Roman occupation Egypt did not change its religion or its language. With the Arab invasion in 641 Egypt changed from being a Christian Egyptian speaking nation into Islamic Arabic speaking, and all happened in less than 250 years. Most of the sultans and rulers were foreign.
How did the Egyptians, the Copts, deal with the invasion, and what is their social situation?

The Copts in Egypt are fourteen to sixteen millions of a population of one hundred millions. Add to that nearly three millions in the USA, Canada, Australia, Europe and other countries.

The history of the Copts is often read only in view of big political or military happenings that take place in the land Egypt. This forms part of the history of the Copts. Besides the fact that the Copts experience the general political or military changes in the country, they have to deal with many regulations and laws that are put only for them as being Copts. Some Western and Egyptian historians have written about the development of the Egyptian Christians during the Greek and the Byzantine periods, and others followed those who remained Christian, the Copts, under the Arab and other Islamic reigns. The historic account you get in this book is compiled out various Western and Egyptian historic sources. These facts tend to serve as an example of a bigger picture and are meant to underline the difficulties and the hardships that the Egyptians, who gradually became Christian minority, Copts, had to endure throughout the ages to the present time to remain Christian.

Since that Alexander the Great seized Egypt in 331 BC and up till the 23rd of July revolution in 1952, which ended the English and the Turkish rule, Egypt was continuously controlled by foreign powers.

It is the year 331 BC

The Greek has a mixed feeling towards this 4000 years old civilisation. According to them, the Egyptians seem to be extremely religious, tend to spirituality and use many symbols. The Greeks remain mainly in the area around Alexandria and build some cities along the Nile. They avoid the countryside but they export the Egyptian grain to their country.

It is the year 31 BC

The Roman Empire forces reach Alexandria, and Cleopatra, who was of Macedonian origin commits suicide. The Greek power ends, but the cultural impact on the country continues for centuries to come.

The first and second century

Centuries before Jesus was born many Bible figures sought refuge in Egypt. Also Jesus with His mother, the Virgin Mary and Joseph fled to Egypt. With this visit the Egyptians identified the goddess Isis with her child Horus, that was worshipped for many centuries, with the Virgin Mary with her Child.

It is nearly 55 years after the birth of Jesus.

The apostle Mark visits Alexandria, and brings Christianity to Egypt He establishes the Coptic Church. The church considers him the first Patriarch.

St Mark in Egypt

It is the year 68 St. Mark is tortured and killed in the streets of Alexandria. Years later, the Byzantine authorities take the body of St. Mark to one of their churches in Alexandria, while the head stays in the main Coptic Church. Years later, some Venetian pirates steel the body and bring it to Venice where they consider him the city patron, and build for him the cathedral of St. Mark in Venice.

A successor is chosen. And from now on, the Patriarchs of the Coptic Church will be at the head of the church for an unbroken line. The present patriarch, pope Tawadros, is the 118th patriarch.

The School of Alexandria

The School of Alexandria, established by St. Mark, is becoming a world wide educational centre. Many Greek and Roman intellectuals, scholars and philosophers are coming to Alexandria for study. It is in the School of Alexandria that Christianity first taught using allegorical and symbolic way of explaining the Biblical texts.

The Byzantine authorities following the example of that of the Roman Empire import grain and other Egyptian products. Ships leave Alexandria heading, not Athens or Rome, but Constantinople.

It is almost 200 years now since St. Mark found his death in the streets of Alexandria. No church is built so far, although the majority of the Egyptians are Christians. In Alexandria the small but strong Jewish and Greek minority continue to live and trade.

Scholars of the School of Alexandria are translating the Old Testament from the Hebrew and the New Testament from the Greek language into the Egyptian. For the first time a complete Bible exists with its two Testaments. In order to make it easy for everybody to read the Bible, the translators used Greek letters in writing the Egyptian language. This Egyptian language written in Greek letters is what we call up till now the Coptic language. Seven Egyptian letters were added, for they did not exist in the Greek alphabet.

The Third Century

It is halfway the third century, and Rome keeps giving orders for killing all Christians and destroying all churches in Egypt. As a result, more than one million Egyptian Christians are killed. In 284 Roman authorities begin the biggest persecution ever taken place. Commemorating this wave of persecution, the Coptic Church starts its calendar in the year 284. It is the Anno Martyros calendar, the Martyrs Calendar.

With the spread of Christianity in Egypt, a new form of Christian life started to take place. Monasticism started in Egypt when increasing number of people was seeking solitary form of life to be with God. This form of life was worldwide known because of St. Antonius who lived alone and later he got many followers. It was then that Egypt presented to the world the main three systems of monastic life. On the other hand, the School of Alexandria presented a fine explanation of the Holy Trinity and assisted in writing the Church creed.

Egypt under the Byzantine Empire

The Fourth Century

It is the fourth century, and the popularity of the monastic life is tremendously increasing. Throughout the width and the breadth of Egypt hundreds of monasteries are built for thousands of monks and nuns.

In France, Germany and even in Ireland there are monasteries built according to the rules of St. Antonius and St. Bachoum. Europe gets to know this new Christian form of life, and many scholars, travellers and interested people come to Egypt to stay for a while in one or more of these monasteries. They start writing the life, sayings and wisdom of the Desert Fathers. One of the people whose life was changed as a result of reading the life story of St. Antonius was St. Augustine.

With great success the Coptic Church participates in the second council of Nicaea in 325 and the third council of Constantinople in 381. The Coptic Church defends the right creed against various heresies. The charismatic pope Athanasius defends the Virgin Mary dogma. The Virgin Mary gets the name Theotokos, mother of God. When Pope Athanasius was sent in exile to the then Roman territory Trier, he wrote the life story of St. Antonius. Soon after, the story was translated to Latin and found its way to all European languages.

The Fifth century

Constantinople, a recognised world power now, is trying to
control both the country and the church. The people support
the church and stand firmly behind their chosen patriarch.
Both Rome and Constantinople have played a very decisive
role during the meetings of the Chalsedon Council. The
Coptic patriarch was exiled and Constantinople sent her own
chosen patriarch to Egypt. Due to the fact that the Copts and
the Coptic Church continue to refuse the foreign patriarch,
the Coptic Church is gradually isolated from other world
churches. Constantinople forces continue confiscating Coptic
churches with its property. Many Coptic churches are put to
fire to intimidate the Copts and to force them to accept the
foreign appointed patriarch.

The Sixth Century

During the sixth century, the Coptic Church was
continuously in conflict with the Byzantine authorities.
Coptic patriarchs were often exiled, and many churches were
confiscated. In the meantime monasteries have become the
source of spirituality and have the function of keeping both
faith and culture alive.

How and when did the Arabs occupy Egypt?

The Seventh Century

While the Byzantine authorities tighten the grip on Egypt,
they lose the war against the new invading nation, the Arabs.

The man in charge of Egypt, Al Moukawkas enjoys not only the military power, but he is also appointed as the head of the church. With both powers in hands he can do whatever he pleases with the country. Losing the war against the Arabs, Al Moukawkas signs the Byzantine capitulation and hands over Egypt to the Arabs

It is 641
The Arabs takes over Egypt. A small growing nation is ruling now one of the oldest civilisations in the world.

The Egyptians during first two centuries of the Arab invasion

Less than forty years after the Arab invasion to Egypt the Arabs imprison the Coptic patriarch because he fails to pay the Gizia, the taxes due on him and his church. The Arabs stipulate new rules for the Copts: From now on no Copt is allowed to ride a horse.
All Copts should have clothes with certain colours. They are obliged to let Arabs live in their homes. Forcing Copts to work for paving streets, building mosques and other civil work has become the rule.
It has become very difficult to get a permission to build a new church, and a permission to restore an existing one has to wait for years.

It is only 50 years since the Arab invasion has taken place. The Copts are forced to learn Arabic to prove that they are not insulting Islam while praying. It is forbidden to talk in Coptic in any of the public places. More and more people convert to Islam for not being able to pay the Gizia, the taxes due on them.

The 8th century
The Alawite dynasty 680-772 AD
Egypt had 25 governors

The present Coptic patriarch has to visit all cities and villages along the Nile to collect money for the taxes. It has always been the only way for all patriarchs to avoid prison and torture. Major reasons behind converting Copts to Islam are the social and financial difficulties. Also the Arabs blindly chose sides with Moslem people and insist on using only the Arabic language.
The new taxes are to be paid on name of all the relatives who are dead. All crosses in and outside churches are destroyed. This applies to icons. The temples of the pharaohs are facing the same fate.

Egypt under the Abbasid Dynasty
750-1258

The ninth century

Since 706 Arabic is the official language of the country:
831

The biggest Coptic rebel against the Arabs has just begun. Although the Caliph El Mamoun uses all possible means to suppress it, the Delta area is a battlefield. It is called Bashmourieen rebel, referring to the wastelands between Demietta and Rosetta Nile branches. Many Moslem Egyptians chose to fight with the Copts against the Arab rulers.

It is the year 847

The reign of Al Mutawakkil forces all Copts to wear a special shawl on their heads and shoulders and a girdle around their waste. Clothes has to be yellow like honey, made as patchwork of small pieces.
Donkeys should have special wooden saddles.
Copts who have a big home are forced to give one tenth of it to build a mosque. If anybody would start building a new church, it will be directly pulled down.
All Copts have to install a wooden pillar in front of their homes. It is called the devils' pillar. The pillar will tell the Moslems if the people living there are Copts or not.
No crosses are to be held high in churches or in public during processions or religious feasts.
Moslem students are not to get lessons from any Coptic teachers. Coptic students are not accepted anymore in a Moslem school.

The tenth century

The Tolonian Dynasty
It is the year 968

Egypt is booking great economic and cultural progress since that Al Muiz has established the Fatimide dynasty.

It is the year 996, and Caliph Al Hakim has started giving the most bizarre orders.
All shoes belonging to women are confiscated to make sure that they would not leave home. Women are not even allowed to look out of windows.
In the meantime all dogs are killed.

All Copts are bound to wear only black clothes. Priests and monks are no more to wear their centuries old white clothes, since black is the colour from now on.
Carpenters are busy producing the five-pound crosses that every male Copt has to wear around his neck. They have to wear the crosses even in bathrooms. Public bathes have now separate areas for Copts.

The Eleventh century

Copts During The Crusades wars

It is almost the end of the eleventh century

1096-1099

The first Crusade campaign is begun.

Moslem Egyptians see that the invaders carry crosses on their chests and they conclude that the Copts will fight side by side the foreign invaders. On the other hand, Rome thinks that the belief of the Copts is full of wrong elements. For Rome the history of the council of Chalcedon in the fifth century is still alive.

The twelfth century

The son of El Hafez, prince Hasan, arrests patriarch Gabriel Ben Terbek, the seventieth Coptic patriarch. The Pope has to pay ransom of 1000 dinar.

The thirteenth century

During the reign of the Fatemides from 969 to 1171,
the Ayoubieeen from 1171 to 1250
and the Bahrain Mamloukes from 1250 to 1390
the majority of the Copts become Moslem.

The fourteenth century

Egypt is suffering from famine since last century. And plague is attacking the country since 1334.
The latest news confirm the fact that the Sunni Olama (The Moslem educated ones) have advised the government to start a campaign to humiliate the Copts who are working in the governmental offices and try to convert them to Islam.

The fifteenth century

In nine years, between 1429 and 1438 thousands of people have died of plagues.

Hundreds of monasteries in Shehiet and elsewhere are burnt and left in ruins. Moslem Egyptians are feeling more and more that the Copts are becoming strangers to them.

The sixteenth century

When Sultan Selim the 1st seizes power in 1517, Egypt fell in the hands of the Ottomans Empire.
For the coming three centuries Egypt will be living in the darkest eras ever occurred. Political, social and financial aspects are deteriorating. As one of the writers notes on the end of the Ottomans rule (the Turks left only the Pyramids behind them).

The seventeenth century

The plagues of 1603,1619, 1626 and 1642 has claimed the life of many.

Patriarch Matheus, following the custom of his predecessors travels to collect the taxes due on the Coptic Church. This time to pay for the taxes on the ceremonies needed for inaugurating the patriarch. Copts had to borrow the needed money from a Jew.

The big church of the city Al Mahalla Al Koubra in Delta is destroyed and an Islamic school in built instead.

There is a new tax on every Copt who leaves him home. In this way most of Copts are under house arrest for they are not able to pay. They cannot go as well to their work or even buy necessities.

The eighteenth century

Egypt is in a state of civil war. Forces of the Mamlukes and the Turkish authorities fight everywhere. Both Moslem and Christians feel unsafe.

Churches in Alexandria are burned and destroyed and many Christians flee the city.

It is almost the end of the eighteenth century. Patriarch Marcus the 8th gets to hear from the Turkish governor that all Copts have to wear special kind of clothes in order to be directly recognised. Anybody refuses will be simply stoned to death.

It is 1798 and the forces of Napoleon arrive in Egypt.

The nineteenth century

Mohamed Ali, who was born on the Macedonian border, seizes power 1805
As usual Copts are not allowed to serve in the army because Moslem Egyptians do not trust them.
When Mohamed Ali sends Moslem students in various scientific scholarships to Europe no Copt is allowed to participate.

Said, grandson of Mohamed Ali abolishes in 1855 the Gizsia, the tax a Copt has to pay for keeping his religion. All Copts have to serve now in the army. Many army officers misuse this rule and many Copts are in great trouble for not wanting to convert to Islam.
For the first time a Copt turns to Catholicism. He was head of the governmental offices. He became Catholic on the request of Mohamed Ali.

End of the century, 1899, the first Catholic Patriarch was appointed from Rome. It was Kyrolos Makar.

Due to the Protestant missionaries to Egypt as from 1854, they succeeded at the end of the century to establish various protestant churches.

In 11 September 1875 the Khedewi Ismail abolished the use of the Coptic calendar which was used parallel with the Islamic calendar.(this corresponds to the first day of the Coptic calendar: 1st Tout, 1592 AM - Anno Martyrum)

The twentieth century

Throughout the centuries, the Copts build up the reputation that they are industrious, zealous for learning and to be trusted. For these reasons they are allowed now to work as treasurers, architects, doctors and administrators. In the first half of the century a high percentage of teachers, professors, doctors chemists, bankers, merchants, and industrial managers were Copts. Nasser socialism in the fifties and the sixties was a strong blow for the capitalist economic system in which Copts played a dominant rule. Copts possessed 75% of the transport concerns. Nationalisation of banks harmed the Coptic capital which formed a major resource for these banks. Land Reform laws were harmful as well. Land was taken from the Copts and was given to the Moslem. Even lands belonged to the Coptic Church was given to the Moslems.

Before the 1952 Revolution, the Copts formed nearly 60 % of the middleclass positions and nearly 90% of the higher ones in the ministry of finance. In 1974 the percentage was 16%.

Nasser appealed to the Moslems of Egypt by propagating that his policy of "Arab socialism" came from the spirit of Islam, and Egypt is part of the Islamic Arab world. This resulted in a growing wave of Islamising many departments in the government and in the civil services. Islamic religion became a condition of appointment and promotion in key positions in the civil services.

Between 1952 and 1973 no single Copt was appointed as ambassador.

Up till the 1970s, the ministry of higher education had no Copt as president or dean of any of the universities or the higher institutes.

A request to build a Coptic university is denied up till now. No Egyptian university has a Coptic department for teaching Coptic language, art or history.

At the moment the general policy is that of putting difficulties and endless procedures to build any church. Attacking and killing innocent people happen sometimes and mostly in the south of Egypt. Also priests and monks are target for attacks. Churches are now and then burned. The smallest clashes between a Moslem and a Copt, is enough to burn a whole village and send many families away.

Now the Copts try to get some problems solved. Among these problems are:

Getting back the church-land taken by the government.

Abolishing the hundreds of years old Turkish law that prohibits building churches.

Having a permission to establish Coptic departments in universities

Allowing university graduate in the public service offices.

Allowing church sermons to be sent on radio and television on feast days.

Copts are to get free day on major feasts

In the old part of Cairo, Babylon, there are twelve churches date from the first centuries. Only the church of Mari Mena was built in the twentieth century during the lifetime of Pope Kyrolos the 6th.

The 21st century

The church is suffering from Islamic fundamentalists, mostly influenced by other Arab Islamic countries. Under the hated Moslem Brotherhood regime of one year, many churches were burnt and discrimination took alarming forms.
Since that president El Sisi is in power, the situation of the Copts is getting better. but still incidents take place and families have to leave homes and settle somewhere else.
For the first time a president visits the Coptic Cathedral on Christmas eve, a thing that president El Sisi did, and was profoundly appreciated among millions of Copts in Egypt and around the world.
Copts gets a free day on the 7th of January, Christmas day. There are some regulations to speed up the building of a church when it is needed.
On the whole, a better Egypt is emerging with a civil cooperation and determination to build the country on democratic basis.

Throughout history, this proud nation has been subjected to many forms of political exploitation, religious discrimination, wealth usurping. This still have a great impact on every one and every thing in the country. Unless Egypt would come to realize its uniqueness and beauty and its deserved place in the world, various outside forces will try to take advantage of it.

And up till now teaching of Hieroglyphic and Coptic languages are not relevant. In this respect, Egypt has cut the link with its past and only by reviving and studying these two heritage languages that Egypt would regain its unique position in the world.

www.ingramcontent.com/pod-product-compliance
Lightning Source LLC
Chambersburg PA
CBHW020943100426
42741CB00006BA/845